Focus on Climate Change

CLIMATE CHANGE STRATEGIES

How We Can Help Our Planet

REBECCA SCHROEDER

TWENTY-FIRST CENTURY BOOKS / MINNEAPOLIS

For professors like Ward, engineers like Alex, regenerative farmers like Allison, and everyone else working to create a more sustainable world.

Twenty-First Century Books™
An imprint of Lerner Publishing Group, Inc.
241 First Avenue North
Minneapolis, MN 55401 USA

For reading levels and more information, look up this title at www.lernerbooks.com.

Main body text set in Bembo Std Regular.
Typeface provided by Monotype Typography.

Library of Congress Cataloging-in-Publication Data

Names: Schroeder, Rebecca author
Title: Climate change strategies : how we can help our planet / Rebecca Schroeder.
Description: Minneapolis, MN : Twenty-First Century Books, [2026] | Series: Focus on climate change | Includes bibliographical references and index. | Audience: Ages 11–18 | Audience: Grades 7–9 | Summary: "Climate change is a pressing issue that impacts everyone. So, how can we slow it down or stop it? From transportation to energy to sustainable habits, dive into different ways to combat climate change"—Provided by publisher.
Identifiers: LCCN 2025011156 (print) | LCCN 2025011157 (ebook) | ISBN 9798765644218 library binding | ISBN 9798348029586 paperback | ISBN 9798348000103 epub
Subjects: LCSH: Climatic changes—Juvenile literature | Greenhouse gases—Environmental aspects—Juvenile literature | Renewable energy sources—Juvenile literature
Classification: LCC QC903.15 .S33 2026 (print) | LCC QC903.15 (ebook) | DDC 363.7/052—dc23/eng/20250609

LC record available at https://lccn.loc.gov/2025011156
LC ebook record available at https://lccn.loc.gov/2025011157

Manufactured in the United States of America
1-1012703-52447-5/5/2025

CONTENTS

INTRODUCTION

In 2023 residents of China's capital city, Beijing, were ordered to stay indoors on two occasions. First, there were the sandstorms. In April, a dangerous orange haze hit Beijing and the rest of northeastern China four times in one month. The air was so heavily polluted with smog and sand that everyone was advised to remain inside. Although sandstorms normally occur in this part of China in the spring, the same deforestation and industrialization that contribute to climate change are worsening the storms.

That same month, people across Asia stayed inside for a different reason: extreme heat. Much of Bangladesh, India, Laos, and Thailand experienced record-high temperatures in April, with highs reaching 113.9°F (45.5°C) in Tak, Thailand. In May, Vietnam recorded its highest-ever temperature of 111.38°F (44.1°C). Then in July China also saw its national high-temperature record broken in the township of Sanbao, where temperatures rose to a sweltering 125.96°F (52.2°C).

In July, residents of Beijing were told to stay indoors for the second time that year. This time, the culprit was more record high temperatures. Temperatures in the city soared to 104°F (40°C), and the Chinese government issued a red alert—the highest warning possible for extreme temperatures—as they ordered companies to stop all outdoor work. Beijing was in the midst of a twenty-seven-day streak of temperatures above 95°F (35°C). But they were not alone.

Record heat in the South American country of Chile and thousands of miles away on Italy's island of Sardinia caused wildfires to break out in both places. The National Oceanic and Atmospheric Administration (NOAA) later confirmed that July 2023 was the hottest July on record and likely Earth's hottest month on record. July 21 also set a new record for the hottest day since at least 1940.

Every month in 2023 from June to September set records for the hottest that month has been to date. In 2024

Fueled by the combination of heat, drought, and windy conditions, wildfires raged across Los Angeles in January 2025 and destroyed hundreds of homes.

scientists declared 2023 to be the hottest on record, with 2024 expected to be even hotter. What's responsible for this extremely hot Earth? The culprit is climate change.

The Time Is Now

Climate change will impact everyone on Earth. The emission of greenhouse gases drives it. These are gases, such as methane and carbon dioxide, that trap heat. As humanity releases more of these gases, the average global temperature rises. In addition to a world that is warmer on average, other effects of climate change include more extreme storms, changed rainfall patterns leading to more droughts and floods, melting glaciers, rising oceans, and more.

Just as the record-breaking heat did in China, Chile, and beyond, the consequences of climate change can displace people from their homes and make it harder for people to survive. It's important to develop strategies to slow down climate change and minimize its effects. Since human-caused greenhouse gas emissions are a major cause of climate change, finding strategies for reducing these emissions is a strong place to start.

Addressing Greenhouse Gas Emissions

There are many sources of greenhouse gas emissions. This means there are many different strategies we can pursue to reduce emissions and slow down climate change. One place to start is the energy sector, which is responsible for 75 percent of the world's greenhouse gas emissions. There are different sections within the energy sector, including transportation, heat and electricity, buildings, manufacturing, and construction, which will require different types of solutions. The other 25 percent of the world's greenhouse gas emissions come from land use changes and sectors such as agriculture. For example, when people chop down a forest to build a housing development, the forest releases greenhouse gases such as carbon dioxide.

Since the energy sector is responsible for the majority of emissions, let's start by examining solutions there.

Large-scale deforestation is a human activity that releases CO_2 into the atmosphere.

CHAPTER ONE

Embracing Renewable Energy

There are a few different ways to reduce the amount of greenhouse gas emissions that come from the energy sector. We can switch the types of energy we use to sources that emit less or no greenhouse gases. We can change the way we design buildings, homes, and appliances so that they require less energy to build and function.

Let's start with where we get energy from. There are two types of sources: renewable and nonrenewable. Renewable energy comes from an unlimited resource that can be naturally replenished—it doesn't run out. No matter how much wind our windmills use to produce energy, there will always be more wind. The tides will continue to flow in and out day after day, even if we use their motion to produce energy. We can't use up the sun, the wind, or the tides. That means wind energy, solar power, and tidal power are all types of renewable energy.

Nonrenewable energy resources are limited. They come from sources that either can't be naturally replenished or would take much longer to replenish than the rate at which we use them. For example, nuclear energy is obtained by splitting the nucleus of atoms. While the technology may exist someday to make nuclear energy renewable, it is currently considered nonrenewable. That's because the process uses the element uranium, and there is a limited amount of uranium on Earth. Once we mine it all, there will be no way to get more.

Fuels including coal, oil, and natural gas are also nonrenewable energy resources. These three are called fossil fuels because they were made in the ground from plant and animal remains. More can technically be made, but they are made over the course of millions of years. So, if we use up all of these resources that we have, we will be out of them.

Fossil fuels such as coal are often found underground. Some of these deposits stretch for hundreds of miles.

Nonrenewable Energy Resources

Why are nonrenewable energy sources harmful? For some, they're not ideal because they involve using up the resource, such as nuclear energy's use of uranium. Mining for uranium also affects ecosystems, and nuclear power plants produce radioactive waste that must be stored away from people and animals for hundreds of thousands of years. However, nuclear energy plants have environmental benefits, too—namely that they produce no greenhouse gas emissions. In contrast, burning fossil fuels releases a massive amount of greenhouse gas emissions.

In the 1800s and 1900s, coal was the dominant energy source used in the United States. Though no longer the dominant source of energy, coal consumption reached a historic peak in 2005. Every 1 ounce (28 g) of coal burned releases 4 ounces (113 g) of carbon dioxide into the atmosphere, which causes respiratory health issues and climate change. Coal-fired power plants also emit harmful air pollutants such as carbon monoxide, mercury, and lead. In addition to air pollution, the process of coal mining harms the environment. People destroy mountaintops and forests to build the mines, and as of 2021, coal mining produced more than 100 million tons (90.7 million t) of toxic waste each year, which must then be stored in pits. The United States' use of coal has been declining since 2005, but in 2022, it still accounted for 19 percent of carbon emissions from the US energy sector and 55 percent of emissions from the electric power sector. Scientists and engineers have developed technologies to reduce emissions of pollutants and make coal more energy efficient, but coal use still releases carbon dioxide and other air pollutants and produces toxic waste.

Natural gas moves around the US in long pipelines such as this one. There are about 3 million miles (4.8 million km) of pipe in the network. The longest pipeline runs from Michigan's Upper Peninsula to south Texas.

Natural gas pipelines first arose in the early 1900s, but it took until 2023 for natural gas to be used to meet half of America's electricity demand. At first glance, natural gas seems like a cleaner fuel than coal. This is because power plants that use natural gas release less carbon emissions than coal-fired power plants. However, natural gas is composed primarily of methane, which is an even more powerful greenhouse gas than coal's carbon dioxide. Natural gas has unique issues, too. For example, significant methane leaks are common when obtaining natural gas and converting it to energy. According to estimates by the US Environmental Protection Agency (EPA), 7.2 million tons (6.5 million t) of methane—equivalent to about 1 percent of all natural gas production—leak each year. And other studies have found this amount to be much higher. So, because of how these leaks contribute to greenhouse gas emissions, it's safe to say that natural gas is not a climate-friendly fuel.

Although the United States successfully reduced carbon emissions from fossil fuels by 3 percent in 2023, global emissions from fossil fuels were still the highest they've ever been. Nonrenewable energy sources power these emissions. So, what are some more sustainable alternatives? Let's explore different types of renewable energy.

Solar Energy

Solar energy can be used for heating or to produce electricity. It's obtained when light from the sun shines onto solar panels. Solar panels use technology called photovoltaic cells, which take light energy and convert it to electrical energy. The process of manufacturing solar panels and obtaining the materials for them still releases greenhouse gas emissions. However, solar panels and power plants that use solar technologies produce no greenhouse gases when they operate. This means that switching from fossil fuels to solar energy significantly reduces emissions.

Solar farms, or large collections of solar panels, reduce carbon dioxide emissions more than having a forest on the same amount of land would. But that doesn't mean we should cut down forests and replace them with solar panels. Forests absorb carbon dioxide as well. Instead, deserts are great places to put solar panels because the land is already mostly bare, and they have a lot of sunny days. The roofs of buildings and houses are also a great place to put solar panels since they are bare and receive more direct sunlight than lower-lying places. Parking lots are another option. Cars can

Solar farms harvest energy from the sun that is then used to produce clean electricity. The largest in the US is in the Mojave Desert and covers 4,660 acres (18.9 sq. km).

park underneath the panels to get shade, and the panels will produce electricity.

One drawback of solar energy is that it takes a lot of different elements and minerals to make solar panels and to make the batteries that store solar energy. This means that while solar energy itself is renewable, the materials required to make solar panels are limited. They also must be mined, which creates greenhouse gas emissions and can pollute surrounding soil, water, and air. Five of the elements required for solar panel production—arsenic, gallium, germanium, indium, and tellurium—are considered seriously endangered elements. This means that our usable supply of these elements is at risk of running out within the century.

Solar Roadways

Named after its central concept, the goal of the company Solar Roadways is to replace normal pavement used to make roads with durable solar panels. These roads would then be able to generate energy. Solar roadways would be able to use some of this energy to melt accumulated ice or snow. They also wouldn't need to be painted with markings and would instead use LED lights. The company built its first prototype, a solar parking lot, in 2011. Since then, they've installed more prototypes and built different versions of the panels using what they've learned from prior models to improve them. The company is first focusing on installing solar panels on sidewalks, driveways, and in parking lots because they haven't done testing on major roads with lots of traffic, such as highways. It's slow progress, and due to issues involving cost and durability (panels are much more expensive and fragile than pavement), this may never be a widespread solution. But it demonstrates the creative solutions to climate change people have and will come up with.

This doesn't mean we shouldn't use solar energy. But to most effectively combat climate change, we will need to use a mix of renewable technologies. Solar energy is an important part of that mix. To help preserve the minerals used to make solar panels, we can recycle the panels at the end of their lives and recover some of the materials. Recycling electronics such as these is also an important way to reduce greenhouse gas emissions. We'll talk about that more in chapter five.

Wind turbines are much bigger than they might seem from far away. The average US wind turbine on land is about 339 feet (103 m) tall. Offshore turbines are even taller.

Wind Energy

Windmills harness wind energy and transform it into electrical energy. Wind energy doesn't emit any greenhouse gases or other pollutants. Unlike many other energy sources, windmills also don't require any water. This makes wind an especially sustainable energy alternative. You'll often see windmills on top of mountains or in valleys where wind is plentiful. You may see offshore wind farms as well, which are windmills constructed in the sea. While offshore wind farms are more costly to build and operate, air currents in the sea are 70 percent stronger than on land. This means that offshore wind farms can create three times the electricity of land-based wind farms.

The only emissions windmills release are related to the materials used in their manufacturing process. However, the amount of emissions released in this process is small compared to fossil fuels. For example, to produce the same amount of electricity, coal releases eighty-eight times more carbon dioxide emissions than wind. Additionally, studies have shown that wind farms can generate enough clean energy in two years to make up for all the greenhouse gas emissions they'll create in their lifetime.

One older drawback to this energy alternative involved the recycling of wind turbine blades, as the technology to recycle them did not exist until 2022. Since then several companies have developed ways to recycle wind turbine blades. In France, the utility company Veolia turns turbine blades into an ingredient used to produce cement, and in Tennessee, the energy-focused development lab Carbon Rivers turns them into glass fibers, which can then be used to make new turbine blades.

Hydroelectric Power

Hydroelectric power, or hydropower for short, uses moving water to generate electrical energy. There are several types of moving water that can be harnessed: ocean tides that rise and fall at least 10 feet (3 m), waterfalls, and flowing rivers. Dams can also create large reservoirs of water, which can then be released slowly over a turbine to generate electricity. Hydropower is one of the oldest sources of renewable energy, and it's been used to generate electricity in the United States since 1880.

The United States generates a lot of hydropower from rivers and dams. The largest tidal power station in the world is in South Korea. Tidal power plants can generate power from both rising and falling tides. Tidal turbines (much like wind turbines), tidal fences, and barrages, which function similarly to dams, all generate power from tides.

The Enguri Dam and Hydro Power Plant in Tsalenjikha, Georgia, were completed in 1978. The dam is one of the highest concrete dams in the world.

The process of generating electricity from hydropower doesn't emit any greenhouse gases. However, obtaining the materials necessary to construct the power plant releases some emissions. Most hydropower projects have low emissions, similar to other sources of renewable energy, but the total amount depends on the project. Around 10 percent of hydropower plants in the world emit as many greenhouse gases per unit of energy as fossil fuel plants emit. The emissions vary so widely because the creation of reservoirs results in bacteria decomposing, or breaking down, organic matter. This process releases carbon dioxide and methane. The location and age of a reservoir impact how much matter is decomposing—and how much gas emissions occur. In general, the hotter the climate and the younger the reservoir, the more emissions will be produced.

Geothermal Power

Geothermal power is generated using heat that comes from the earth. It's generally harnessed around hot springs, volcanoes, geysers, and the edges of tectonic plates. Anywhere there is heat underground close to Earth's surface, a power plant can be constructed to convert that energy into useful heat energy or even into electricity. In the United States, there are many geothermal power plants located in western states, such as California, Idaho, and Colorado, and some in Alaska and Hawaii.

Geothermal power plants are a strong alternative energy source for reducing emissions. A geothermal plant will emit 99 percent less carbon dioxide than a fossil fuel power plant of a similar size. They also have very little negative impact on the environment. The worst of these impacts is that geothermal power plants can release toxic heavy metals, such as arsenic, mercury, and nickel, into the water. They can also release hydrogen sulfide, which can be harmful to people with respiratory illnesses.

Recycling is common in this industry. Many geothermal power plants inject the steam and water that they use back into the earth so it can be used again for geothermal energy in the future. The only drawback of this type of energy is that not every location is ideal for obtaining it. The best spots for geothermal plants are areas along tectonic plate boundaries, such as the Ring of Fire (a tectonic plate boundary bordering much of the eastern Asian and European coasts and western North and South American coasts). This makes, for example, western North and South America excellent locations for geothermal plants, while the eastern United States and the entire country of Brazil in eastern South America are not viable locations.

Green Building

Another approach to limiting greenhouse gas emissions is to reduce the amount of energy we need. In our daily lives, buildings are some of the largest users of energy. Globally, the operation of buildings accounts for 26 percent of greenhouse gas emissions from the energy sector. Of this 26 percent, 18 percent of emissions are due to electricity and heating used in buildings. Let's look at some ways we can reduce the amount of energy buildings need.

Some people are embracing passive building principles. These are strategies that rely on the environmental surroundings to control temperature—for example, relying

Powering buildings causes about 30 to 40 percent of total greenhouse gas emissions worldwide.

on shade and good insulation instead of an air conditioner to keep a house cool. Passive houses—buildings designed using these principles—are much more efficient in heating or cooling and use a fraction of the energy that regular buildings need. Specifically, the International Passive House Association says that to be considered a passive home, "a house must consume 86 percent less energy for heating and 46 percent less for cooling compared with other code-compliant buildings in the same climate."

Strategies for accomplishing this vary depending on the climate where the house is located. In general, the house should get a lot of shade in the summer when it's hotter and a lot of sun in the winter when it's colder. Thicker-than-normal insulation made of high-quality materials and multi-pane windows are usually used to minimize heat transfer between the house and the outdoors. The insulation and windows are installed carefully so that there are no places where air can leak outside. While passive homes are popular in Europe, as of 2023, there were only 250 certified passive buildings in the United States. But as climate change worsens, passive houses are becoming more popular in the United States as well.

In addition to passive building principles, larger buildings may adopt green roofs to save energy. A green roof is a roof that has soil, vegetation, and sometimes a garden on top of it. Some green roofs are even converted into rooftop parks. These provide a green space where people can walk and relax. This is especially important in cities, which don't have as many green spaces as rural or suburban areas.

Green roofs can help with greenhouse gas emissions in two ways. First, they insulate the building and reduce the amount of energy required to heat and cool it. Second, plants

All kinds of plants, including grass, shrubs, and even trees, can grow on green roofs.

absorb carbon dioxide. Putting plants in an area that would have otherwise been bare helps pull carbon dioxide from the surrounding atmosphere. As an added benefit, green roofs in cities help counteract the heat island effect. This is when cities and urban places have a higher temperature than surrounding areas. The higher temperature is due to several factors. Human structures, such as cars and buildings, emit heat. Large amounts of concrete and asphalt do, too, absorbing heat during the day and slowly releasing it at night. Other factors include the large amounts of air pollution, which can trap heat, in cities and tall buildings that prevent airflow. Another factor is the lack of green spaces and bodies of water in cities, since these help to make it cooler by releasing water vapor into the air. The air temperature around green roofs is 30°F to 40°F (16.7°C to 22.2°C) cooler than it is around normal roofs in cities.

CHAPTER TWO

Low Carbon Transportation

The transportation sector is responsible for 20 percent of global emissions and 28 percent of emissions in the United States. Within the transportation sector, light-duty vehicles (which include the cars that people drive) are responsible for 57 percent of emissions, medium and heavy-duty trucks contribute 23 percent, aircraft 9 percent, ships and boats 3 percent, and rail 2 percent. Studies show that emissions from long-distance trucking, airplanes, and ships will be the most difficult to eliminate. Since they're the easiest to address, we'll start by discussing normal, light-duty car emissions. This area of transportation is also where individuals can make the most impact.

PZEVs

One strategy for addressing light-duty emissions is to replace traditional gasoline-powered vehicles with those featuring more environmentally friendly technologies. This has already been done with the introduction of PZEVs, or partial zero-emission vehicles. These vehicles include easy-to-manufacture accommodations that drastically reduce the emission of harmful, polluting gases. These accommodations include several features that trap or destroy harmful gases to prevent them from leaking into the surrounding air. PZEV cars have fuel system liners, additional carbon canister scrubbers, and a carbon air intake trap, which all stop gas vapor from leaking out of the vehicle. They also contain multiple catalytic converters, which convert pollutants that cause smog and acid rain into less harmful gas emissions. By 2025 all cars sold in the United States will automatically include PZEV technology.

While PZEVs are much better for the environment than other gas-powered cars, they still run on gasoline. This means that they still emit carbon dioxide and contribute to global warming and climate change. To have a vehicle with zero carbon emissions, it would need to be completely electric and not run on gasoline at all.

The Volkswagen Beetle Convertible 2.5 L PZEV is a popular electric car.

Hybrid-Electric Vehicles

Hybrid-electric vehicles, or just hybrids, run on gasoline and electric power. When driving at low speeds, they can get energy from a battery instead of solely burning gas, and they even generate extra energy from friction to store in that battery when the car is braking. There are also newer models called plug-in hybrids. These models never have to be plugged in, but if they are, they can run on only electricity for up to 50 miles (80 km). Hybrid buses are becoming more common as well.

Demand for hybrid vehicles is at an all-time high, with sales increasing 93 percent in 2021 and another 56 percent in 2023. One reason for their increasing popularity is that their combined power sources mean they get high gas mileage. For example, the 2023 Toyota Prius gets 57 miles (92 km) per gallon of gasoline. This is more than double what most gas-powered cars achieve.

However, many environmentalists argue that hybrid cars should not be viewed as the sole solution to climate change. This is because the carbon emissions from hybrid vehicles are still high. In its lifetime, the average gasoline- or diesel-powered vehicle emits somewhere around 43 to 45 tons (39 to 41 t) of carbon dioxide. In comparison, the typical hybrid emits around 36.4 tons (33 t). While plug-in hybrids were first thought to reduce emissions significantly, follow-up studies have shown that they still tend to emit around 31 tons (28 t) of carbon dioxide in their lifetimes. So, while hybrid cars are still better for the environment than traditional cars, there are other options to explore for reducing transportation emissions, too.

Electric Vehicles

While hybrid cars reduce some of the transportation-based greenhouse gas emissions that contribute to climate change, all-electric cars reduce them significantly. Electric vehicles do not burn gasoline at all; instead, they run purely on electricity. This means that as they operate, they don't emit any carbon dioxide. However, the vehicles have batteries inside them, which must be plugged in and charged every so often. If the electricity used to charge electric vehicles comes from fossil fuels, then electric cars still have a carbon footprint.

The process of building electric vehicles also emits more carbon than building traditional vehicles. However, electric vehicles make up for this in just over two years of operating. In this amount of time, the electric vehicle will have reduced

Part of the emissions from building electric vehicles come from manufacturing lithium-ion batteries. These batteries require mined materials and can release toxic chemicals when disposed of at the end of their life.

as much carbon dioxide emissions as a gas vehicle would have emitted from its production and operation. Plus, as of 2024, most batteries for US electric cars are made in other countries with less strict emission standards. When companies move battery production to the United States, as they're required to by the Inflation Reduction Act of 2022, US emissions standards should result in fewer emissions from US electric cars and make them an even better choice.

Electric vehicles are already making a small impact on US carbon emissions. Their popularity has skyrocketed, with electric vehicle sales breaking records in 2022 after increasing more than two-and-a-half times from 2018. To keep up with demand, the United States built the third-largest network of electric vehicle chargers in the world as of 2023. As of 2024, twelve US states are planning to ban the sale of gas-powered cars by 2035, so chances are electric vehicles will play a large role in a more sustainable future.

Promoting Sustainable Transportation Infrastructure

We can also reduce transportation emissions in our daily lives by using cars less overall. One way to do this is to use public transit. Taking the bus or subway to school or work instead of driving a car can reduce the amount of carbon dioxide emitted per trip by about 55 percent. According to the Center for Neighborhood Technology, "public transit in the US saved 63 million metric tons [69 million tons] of carbon dioxide equivalent emissions in 2018—the equivalent of taking 16 coal power plants offline for a year." If this isn't currently possible where you live, you can encourage your local government to increase the amount of public transportation available. You can also ask them to provide incentives for people to use it. For example, a government could provide free or discounted bus or train passes. Another way to use cars less is to walk or bike when possible.

Maglev Trains

In addition to taking public transportation, prioritizing improving it can help fight climate change. One way to do this is to make greener public transportation, such as electric trains. If new and better trains were developed, people may choose to go by train for long-distance trips instead of by car or aircraft.

Original trains were powered directly by coal, but new trains tend to be diesel-electric or electric. Diesel-electric trains can travel up to 134 miles (215 km) per gallon of

A German BR 415 ICE-T electric high-speed train streaks through the Main River Valley in Himmelstadt, Germany.

History of Electric Vehicles

While it may seem like the popularity of electric cars began with the rise of car manufacturers such as Tesla, it turns out that "electric vehicles were some of the earliest automobiles ever invented." Robert Anderson invented the first-ever electric vehicle in 1832, but its battery was only good for one charge before it needed to be replaced. This meant that electric cars didn't become truly practical until at least the 1870s after the first rechargeable batteries were invented. Then in 1901 Ferdinand Porsche invented the world's first hybrid-electric car. As of 2024 only 7.6 percent of cars sold in the United States are electric cars, but at the world's first car show in the year 1900, one-third of the vehicles present were electric.

Electric cars were extremely popular at one point—so what happened to them? With the invention of Ford's Model T in 1908 and the discovery of a large amount of cheap oil in Texas in 1901, gasoline-powered vehicles became a lot cheaper and more popular. By the mid-1930s, electric cars were essentially gone from the roads. They didn't start becoming popular again until the 1970s when gas prices climbed through the roof due to global conflicts. With the challenge of climate change to overcome, electric cars are surging in popularity again.

The Ford Model T is widely considered to be the first car that was affordable for the average middle-class American.

fuel, which makes them a lot more efficient than most cars. Around the world, high-speed trains all tend to be electric. Like electric cars, these result in no greenhouse gas emissions while operating but can still cause some greenhouse gas emissions if the power plant that produces them gets its electricity from fossil fuels.

One innovative type of train technology is the Maglev train. Maglev stands for magnetic levitation. This means that the train hovers above the track using magnets instead of traversing the track on wheels. Maglev trains are considered to use much less energy and greatly reduce greenhouse gas emissions compared to other types of trains. They're also cheaper than other trains to operate and maintain, and they are less likely to leave the track. One drawback is that they can't be integrated into existing railroads, so they require entirely new tracks and stations to be built. Still, countries including Japan, South Korea, and China all have working Maglev railroads and plans to develop more.

CHAPTER THREE

Carbon Capture and Storage Technologies

So far, we've focused mainly on ways to reduce carbon dioxide emissions. Another approach to combating carbon emissions and climate change is to focus on capturing the emissions—either directly from the atmosphere or as they are released from places such as coal-fired power plants—and storing them. The less carbon dioxide we have in the atmosphere, the less it will be able to trap heat and cause climate change.

Methods for Capturing Carbon

Generally, carbon capture and storage (CCS) technologies require three steps. The carbon dioxide is captured, and then it is transported before being stored. There are different points at which you can capture carbon: before it is burned, after it burns, or directly from the air. The first two involve capturing carbon while it is in the process of being used or emitted, perhaps in a factory or power plant. The last one, through a process known as direct air capture (DAC), involves taking carbon dioxide from the atmosphere at any point.

After it's captured, the carbon dioxide is then transported at high pressure using pipes. High pressure makes that transportation cost-effective and efficient. Then, the carbon dioxide is stored in such a way that it can't leak back out into the atmosphere. This storage is called carbon sequestration. There are two ways to sequester carbon—biologically and geologically. Biologically, carbon is stored in plants and soils. If you've ever planted a tree, you're helping to capture carbon dioxide from the atmosphere and store it! Geologically, we can store carbon deep in the ocean or deep underground. Useful locations include porous sedimentary rock and old, empty oil or gas reserves.

When carbon is stored geologically in rock, two things can happen. It can either be simply stored or it can be mineralized. A lot of CCS projects involve injecting the captured carbon into a layer of porous sedimentary rock. This is sequestration—the carbon is only being stored there. Porous rock has tiny spaces or holes through which the carbon dioxide can enter the rock formation. But we don't want the rock to continue to be porous all the way to the surface of Earth because then the carbon dioxide could escape back into the atmosphere. So, this layer of porous rock must have what's known as a caprock above it.

A caprock is a type of rock that prevents the stored carbon from rising and reentering the atmosphere. So, to store carbon we must find a large amount of porous rock with an impermeable rock naturally located above it to act as a caprock. An effective caprock will not allow the gas stored in the porous rock to pass through it. Being impermeable means the caprock

Hoodoos are tall, narrow rock formations that develop when a layer of softer rock is topped by a harder, more erosion-resistant caprock.

will not allow the gas stored in the porous rock to pass through it. It should fit well with the surrounding rock layers to prevent leaks. It also must be able to withstand high pressure without breaking. The high pressure comes from the gas pushing on it from below. The most common types of caprocks include shale, mudstone, gypsum, salt, and certain types of limestone.

Mineralization is a type of permanent storage that doesn't require a caprock. To be mineralized, carbon gas is injected into specific types of igneous rocks that contain alkaline minerals. Basalt (which contains iron, magnesium, and calcium) and peridotites (which contain iron and magnesium) work best. There, the gas undergoes a series of chemical reactions. These reactions convert it into a solid mineral. As a solid mineral, carbon will not be able to enter or reenter the atmosphere. Carbon mineralization is a natural process that happens over the course of millions of years, but scientists can speed it up for CCS. These quicker processes can happen over the course of years or even hours, depending on factors including the type of minerals, temperature, and humidity.

New Potential for Mineralization

Carbon mineralization is a newer type of CCS technology with strong potential. Scientists estimate that with continued research and testing, we'll be able to remove 1 gigaton (1 billion t) of carbon dioxide from the atmosphere by 2035 and 10 gigatons (10 billion t) by 2050. This is significant because 10 gigatons would be a fourth of 2024's total global emissions. Looking even further into the future at the amount of eligible basalt rocks, one study by Icelandic scientist Sandra Ó. Snæbjörnsdóttir and her colleagues found that there is enough storage potential using carbon mineralization to store all the carbon that humans emit. However, it will require a lot of research on effective practices and how to do it in different conditions. Financial investment and research to make the technology more cost-effective will also be necessary to reach that point.

There are other benefits associated with carbon mineralization, too. Mineralized carbon dioxide can be injected into concrete, which strengthens the concrete and allows for less cement to be used when making it. Carbon mineralization even has the potential to use up harmful byproducts from mining, such as asbestos, and turn them into harmless minerals. This is because asbestos tailings—a waste product from asbestos mines that is hazardous to human health—are able to mineralize carbon dioxide by reacting with it to form harmless magnesium carbonate minerals.

Basalt rock formations are the most effective for the carbon mineralization process.

Promoting Investment in CCS

In 2019 the Global CCS Institute, an international company seeking to speed up the creation and use of CCS technology, reported that 44 million tons (40 million t) of carbon dioxide were captured and stored, and this number rose to 48.5 million tons (44 million t) in 2021. This might seem like a lot, but scientists estimate that we need to remove 9.1 billion tons (8.3 million t) of carbon dioxide from the atmosphere every year in order to halt global temperature rise at 1.5°C (2.7 °F) and limit the effects of climate change. This means that the way scientists are using carbon capture and storage can't completely tackle climate change on its own. But it can be a vital solution alongside other strategies. In fact, research by the International Energy Agency suggests

Carbon Cap and Trade Systems

Carbon cap and trade is an economic method to reduce carbon emissions. It caps allowed greenhouse gas emissions. This cap becomes stricter over time. The government sets the cap, and each industry has its own allowed amount of emissions. The cap is then split into how much emissions are allowed per company. The government determines each "number of allowances" and the penalties for going beyond each company's allotment. If companies go beyond their allowance, they could be fined. This gives companies a financial reason to try to emit less carbon dioxide.

Trade comes into this method because companies can sell their allowances if they already emit less than their allowed amount. This means that companies with a lot of emissions will be stuck buying allowances, while companies with few emissions can make extra money, rewarding them for their efforts. In 1995 cap and trade helped significantly reduce the amount of sulfur dioxide in the atmosphere, which is why acid rain isn't as much of an issue as it was before then. Due in large part to the cap-and-trade program, the amount of sulfur dioxide in the air decreased 95 percent from 1980 to 2023.

that CCS technologies will be responsible for 19 percent of the emissions reductions necessary to reach global reduction targets by 2050.

Additionally, there are many promising new technologies, including the carbon mineralization we discussed and ocean-based CCS. With continued funding and support for research and testing, these technologies can make CCS an even greater tool for emissions reduction.

CHAPTER FOUR

Sustainable Agricultural Practices

Changes in the agricultural and food sectors can also help reduce carbon emissions. Within these sectors, the main cause of emissions is deforestation, followed by livestock manure, household consumption, food waste, and fossil fuel use. Collectively, these parts of the agricultural and food sectors are responsible for 31 percent of the world's greenhouse gas emissions. Additionally, emissions from the food supply chain are getting worse over time. In many countries, the food supply chain—which includes processing, packaging, storage, transport, retail, and consumption of food—is set to overtake farming as the largest source of greenhouse gas emissions from the agriculture and food sectors as of the early 2020s.

You can help address emissions from the food supply chain. Buying food locally and when it's in season reduces your food's carbon emissions because it doesn't travel far to reach you. You can buy food locally at farmers markets or through community-supported agriculture (CSA) programs.

Adopting more sustainable farming practices is another important step in fighting climate change. Traditional agriculture might clear forests, often uses a lot of pesticides, and focuses on growing just one crop (monocropping). These practices tend to weaken the soil, reducing both the nutrients needed to sustain crops and its ability to store carbon.

Sustainable Farming Practices

Organic farming does not use pesticides or fertilizers that are produced from fossil fuels. This results in fewer harmful emissions compared to agriculture that relies on these substances. One study that took place over forty years showed that organic farms used 45 percent less energy than traditional ones. Additionally, studies indicate that if people stopped using human-made nitrogen fertilizers, emissions from farms could be reduced by 20 percent. Pesticides also damage soil quality by harming the organisms that live within it. Damaged soil can't store as much carbon dioxide. Some studies suggest that if organic farming became the standard worldwide, farmed soil could actually absorb more carbon than the entire farming industry emits.

Regenerative agriculture is a practice that goes beyond organic farming. It aims to actively heal and restore nature while growing food. Regenerative methods can result in more food grown with less energy, and they also promote healthier soil, which can store more carbon. One method involves planting what are known as cover crops during the times of year when a farmer's main crop isn't growing. This helps maintain the soil by protecting it from wind and rain, which can cause the soil to erode. Cover crops also help

Some experts believe that the spread of organic farming worldwide may lead to soil that can absorb more carbon than is released by the entire agriculture industry.

distribute nutrients to the soil, and their roots prevent soil from becoming compacted, so it's easier to till later, easier for plant roots to take hold, and will hold more nutrients. Additionally, cover crops naturally control weeds so that farmers don't have to use chemical weed killers. Another regenerative method requires farmers to stop tilling the soil because although this makes it easier to plant crops, disturbing the soil also releases carbon dioxide.

Agroforestry is another practice associated with regenerative agriculture. It involves planting native tree species on farmland. Some studies suggest that this simple action could have more impact on the agricultural sector's emissions than anything else. Trees store carbon, so planting more of them removes more carbon dioxide from the atmosphere. Planting

CSAs and Farmers Markets

Local farmers markets usually take place once a week or once a month, especially during summer. They're places for local farmers to gather and sell their products. At these markets, you can find all sorts of local vegetables, fruit, honey, and sometimes even food prepared with local ingredients or handmade goods such as mittens and scarves.

A CSA is basically like getting a subscription to one or more local farms. If you join a CSA, you'll get a box of fresh produce each week. What's included depends on the season, and some CSAs allow you to choose exactly what produce you receive and how much. Some CSAs will deliver the boxes straight to your door, and others will have a location to pick them up nearby.

Depending on where you are and the time of year, a CSA might offer tomatoes, zucchini, herbs, and more.

trees on farms can also enrich the soil and enhance crop production. If the trees are native to the area, they will require less water, fertilizer, and maintenance while also contributing to soil health and improving soil structure.

Permaculture is another agricultural practice that can help reduce emissions. Permaculture's main principle is caring for Earth and its inhabitants and sharing surplus food to eliminate food waste. Permaculture's techniques are similar to those of organic farming and often result in more nutritious and a greater amount of crops than those produced by conventional agriculture. One technique used in permaculture is companion planting, which plants combinations of crops that benefit each other while growing. Similarly, polyculture involves growing several different species of crops in the same space to mimic the diversity of ecosystems that occur naturally. Both of these techniques increase a crop's resilience to pests.

Sugarcane grows alongside rows of cabbage and cauliflower in an example of companion planting.

CHAPTER FIVE

Recycling, Upcycling, and Thrifting

Reducing waste and recycling are important ways to reduce a community's or individual's environmental impact. Methane accounts for 16 percent of global emissions and 30 percent of the global temperature rise since the 1800s. Globally, the waste industry was the fourth largest methane emitter in 2021 and was responsible for a fifth of all methane emissions. Reports show that better recycling, composting, and separation of waste types can cut the sector's emissions by 84 percent. But addressing emissions from the waste sector is often overlooked; more than 25 percent of countries have left it out of their climate action plans.

Landfills and trash incinerators tend to be the largest sources of methane emissions for cities. In response, there's a global movement for cities and individuals to become zero-waste. Being zero-waste involves producing as little waste as possible and trying to compost, recycle, or reuse any waste that is produced. The idea of zero-waste began in the 1970s with Paul Palmer, founder of the Zero Waste Institute. It turned into a movement in the early 2000s when a Zero Waste Conference took place in New Zealand, and an organization—the Zero Waste International Alliance—was formed. Groups like this, as well as individuals, are pushing for people and communities to embrace the concept.

Food waste makes up the largest amount of waste in landfills. One way to strive toward zero waste is to compost as many food scraps or other waste as possible. You can also try to produce less waste to begin with. To do so, avoid buying items that can only be used once, such as single-use plastic water bottles. If you buy a reusable bottle instead, it can be used time and time again. Bringing reusable bags to the store can also avoid the use of plastic. Plastic products create greenhouse gas emissions in every step of their

Every year, between 30 and 40 percent of the US food supply ends up in landfills. That's about 60 million tons (54.4 t) of food annually.

production, including when they're thrown away, so trying to avoid them when possible is an important step in reducing waste-based emissions. Another way to produce less waste is to repair things when they're broken. If your phone's battery stops charging well or your screen has a crack, it can be tempting just to trash it and buy the latest model. Instead, fix the battery or the screen and keep your current phone to reduce your waste.

Recycling

It's estimated that recycling has the potential to reduce carbon emissions by 10.4 to 11.2 gigatons (10.4 billion to 11.2 billion t) of carbon dioxide—as much as what Japan, the world's sixth largest emitter, produces in a year. So many types of waste can be recycled and turned into something new. Recycling also saves energy because it means we don't have to spend extra energy to extract new materials. For example, making an aluminum can out of recycled aluminum scraps saves 95 percent of the energy required to make a brand-new one. This is important because making just forty brand-new aluminum cans uses the same amount of energy as using 1 gallon (4 L) of gas. As for plastic, recycling just ten bottles saves enough energy to power a laptop for twenty-five hours. For paper, seventeen trees can be saved (and can continue absorbing carbon dioxide) for every 1 ton (.9 t) of paper recycled.

Most people know that glass, aluminum cans, plastic, cardboard, and paper can be recycled. But there are many other things that can be recycled that people may not think about. These include batteries, electronics, plastic shopping bags (which usually must be recycled separately from other plastics), lightbulbs, eyeglasses, foam packing, printer ink cartridges, phones, and crayons.

You can recycle electronics, including TVs, computers, phones, radios, cameras, appliances, and more, at certain stores such as Best Buy. Recycling electronic waste is especially important. According to the United Nations, only 17.4 percent of electronics are recycled. But many electronics use metals that must be mined from the earth. It takes a lot more energy to mine more metals than to extract ones that are already present in our electronics for reuse.

Before you throw anything in the trash, it's important to see if it can be recycled instead. For special items such as crayons, you can find information online about where to recycle them. If you're not sure about more basic items such as paper, you can always check online or contact your local

Electronic waste waits to be processed at a recycling center.

Local Recycling Centers

If you can't recycle something in your bin, there's a chance you can recycle it at a local recycling center. You can search online for recycling centers near you. Earth911 has a website that allows you to search for recycling centers that take items you can't put in curbside bins, such as batteries, paint, yard waste, and all sorts of household items, from mattresses to bicycles to flip-flops.

Want to take recycling a step further? Once you've identified recycling centers near you, call them and see if they need volunteers. Volunteering can include helping to sort recyclables or attending events and educating people on how to recycle and what can be recycled. If you can't find any opportunities through recycling centers, try checking local environmental nonprofits or the National Recycling Coalition.

Paint should never go into a landfill. It can be recycled in many places, but you will likely need to box it up and take it to the facility.

government. They'll tell you what items you can put in your recycling bin. It's also important to only put items that can be recycled in that bin. If you put non-recyclable items there, it can cause damage to your local recycling center's equipment and raise the cost of recycling, as it takes extra time to sort these items out.

Thrifting, Upcycling, and Repairing

Making clothes uses 20.9 trillion gallons (79 trillion L) of water per year, and the fashion industry produces 1.18 tons (1.1 million t) of carbon dioxide emissions annually. This means that, when possible, it's better to repair your clothes than buy new ones. Try sewing or patching holes and replacing buttons rather than scrapping the outfit in favor of a new one. If you do buy new clothes, try to find companies with sustainable standards. You can also try to buy clothing with more sustainable fabric. Organic or recycled cotton, hemp, linen, and Tencel are better fabrics for the environment than polyester, acrylic, rayon, and nylon.

Rather than buying new clothes every time you need some, you can try buying clothes that are new to you. This is called thrifting. Thrift shops sell clothes and other objects that people have previously owned, but maybe they no longer fit, or the original owner no longer wanted them. Rather than throwing your old clothes away, donate your clothes to a thrift shop. Instead of browsing stores filled with new clothes at the mall, try heading to a thrift store for some fun shopping with your friends.

You can also upcycle old clothes or similar items. Upcycling means turning something into a new product of equal or greater value to the original. For example, cardboard can be upcycled into new cardboard, or it can be downcycled into paper bags. Paper can be recycled into new paper, or it can be downcycled into toilet paper or paper towels. You can do this on your own, too. Try turning an old glass jar into a vase for flowers or even into a planter for herbs!

On top of recycling, thrifting, and reducing waste, there are other actions we can take to reduce our carbon footprints.

Refinishing or repainting old furniture is a kind of upcycling.

CHAPTER SIX

Daily Sustainability

Sustainability has many definitions. It involves meeting the needs of the present while ensuring that the needs of the future can still be met. Sustainability considers the use of resources and makes sure that we can replenish what we use. In the context of climate change, sustainability means keeping greenhouse gas emissions to a minimum and transforming different sectors of society—such as the energy, transportation, and agricultural sectors—so that they don't contribute to global warming. As individuals, how can we practice sustainability?

Sustainable Living Practices

We know that using less energy is one approach to reducing emissions. There are many ways to conserve energy in your daily life. One way is to use Energy Star certified appliances in your home. These are appliances from any brand that are certified by the EPA to use less energy. Some Energy Star rated appliances include washers, dryers, water heaters, thermostats, ceiling fans, light fixtures, and even computers!

According to the International Energy Agency, government policies on appliance efficiency around the globe have already cut emissions from appliances in half. Countries with strict energy efficiency programs have seen a decrease between 7 percent and 10 percent in energy-related emissions. You can do your part by encouraging your caregivers to consider buying energy-efficient appliances when they need new ones and encouraging your local, state, or national government to adopt even stronger energy policies.

Most people know that conserving water is good for the environment, but they don't know that it reduces greenhouse gas emissions, too. This is because it takes energy to move

Waiting for a full load before running the dishwasher is one way to help conserve water and energy.

water, especially to dry places. Energy star rated products help save water. But you can make an impact, too. You can turn off the water when you're brushing your teeth and wait to do laundry or run the dishwasher until you have a full load. Heating water uses energy, too, so shorter showers and doing laundry in cold water help reduce your emissions.

Another way to save water is to plant drought-resistant plants in your yard or garden. It's even better if the plants are native to your area. Many American yards are full of short grass and not much else. This grass doesn't absorb carbon dioxide nearly as well as other plants would. Native shrubs are a great solution because they have particularly large root systems. They are especially important in areas prone to wildfires and regions such as parts of the Midwest where old-growth forests aren't common. Shrubs are durable, absorb a lot of carbon, and promote healthy soil. Some shrubs even help nearby trees grow better. Native grasses will also absorb a lot of carbon in areas where forests aren't common. In general, the larger the root system, the better the plant is for the soil and for absorbing carbon.

Sustainable Consumption Practices

As mentioned in chapter four, the food supply chain is responsible for a lot of the agricultural industry's emissions. There are many simple actions you can take to reduce your diet's carbon footprint.

Eliminating food waste goes a long way. Studies have shown that "if food waste was a country, it would be the third highest emitter of greenhouse gases after the US and China." About half the food produced in the United States isn't even eaten. It can be difficult not to create any food waste at all. So,

Grow Your Own Food

Growing your own food is a great way to reduce carbon emissions from the food supply chain. Food that you buy at the grocery store may have come from another state or even another country! Growing your own food can eliminate the greenhouse gas emissions associated with transporting your food. Whether you have an outdoor garden or an indoor windowsill garden, there are plenty of great vegetables to grow at home. Lettuce, green beans, zucchini, tomatoes, peas, carrots, cucumbers, spinach, and beets are considered some of the easiest vegetables to grow in an outdoor garden. Herbs such as basil, mint, dill, cilantro, and parsley are easy to grow in pots indoors if you don't have room outside. Head to your local gardening center to buy some seeds and try them out!

If you grow some of your food at home, not only can it be a fun project, but it helps the environment, too.

when you do have food waste, try composting it if you can. Composting results in just 14 percent of the emissions the waste would have created if thrown in a landfill. This is because greenhouse gases, including methane, are formed when food rots in a landfill. If you have a yard, starting a compost pile is a great way to reduce your emissions. You can compost fruit and vegetable scraps as well as eggshells. If you don't have a yard, you can buy or make a compost bin for your kitchen counter or your freezer.

You can also adjust what you eat and how you cook it. More than half of food production emissions come from animal products, especially beef. When cows and sheep digest, they emit methane. Eating less meat—in general, by going meat-free a day or two every week or even by adopting a vegan or vegetarian diet—can help reduce your carbon footprint. For vegetables, 80 percent of emissions come from how they're cooked. For example, cooking them in the microwave uses much less energy than in the oven. On the other hand, up to 70 percent of fruit is consumed raw. Growing conditions and transportation distance are the biggest factors contributing to fruit's carbon footprint. So, buying more local, in-season fruit can help reduce those emissions.

Fruit often travels in greenhouse gas-emitting trucks, impacting its carbon footprint.

CONCLUSION

Building a Greener Future Together

Climate change will impact everyone, so it's important that everyone works to combat it. It's possible to take action on your own or with your family, in your home or in your community, and more. Individual actions are very important in fighting climate change. For example, to help encourage investment in and adoption of renewable energy, individuals can write to their local and state government representatives. They can also educate others on the benefits of renewable energy and how important it is in the fight against climate change. In addition, they can even install solar panels in their homes or talk to their power provider about getting their home's energy from renewable sources. Switching from nonrenewable fossil fuels to renewable sources will go a long way in helping combat climate change. Even though renewable energy sources require mining elements and minerals whose supplies are dwindling, studies show that we have enough of these materials available on Earth to power the entire world with renewable energy. All that's left is for us to do it!

There are also options to join other young people in taking action against climate change, or you can even start your own movement. Here are some examples:

- Take part in the Plastic Free July movement. This group will give you resources to help you reduce or eliminate your plastic waste.
- Join Plant for the Planet in its goal of bringing back a trillion trees or become a Climate Justice Ambassador at one of their academies for young people.
- If you're interested in making a change on a policy level, check out Mock COP. Modeled after the United Nations Conference of the Parties, they are mobilizing a global

Planting trees is just one of many climate-friendly activities you can participate in to help the environment.

movement of young people to help implement positive climate actions.

- The Sunrise Movement is a climate activism-focused group that offers ways to get involved in your community.

You can find information about all these movements and more online. If you can't find any groups to join near you, then start one! Maybe you could begin a recycling club or a gardening club at your school or through your local community center. It's important to help projects and organizations keep running. It's also important to start new projects if you find a new way to promote climate change prevention in your community.

You Can Make a Difference

There are so many smaller, daily ways you can reduce emissions, too—using public transportation, recycling, upcycling, conserving water and energy, growing your own food, and more! Every mile walked rather than driven, and every bottle recycled matters. Perhaps most importantly, you can educate your family and friends about what you've learned about climate change reduction and learn more together. It's more fun changing the world when you can do it together.

GLOSSARY

agroforestry: land management involving the growing of trees in association with food crops or pastures

caprock: an overlying rock layer that is hard to penetrate. This stops stored carbon dioxide from escaping.

carbon footprint: the amount of greenhouse gases, specifically carbon dioxide, emitted by something (such as a person's activities or a product's manufacture and transport) during a given period

climate: the average course or condition of the weather at a place, usually over a period of years, as shown by temperature, wind velocity, and precipitation

combustion: a rapid chemical process, including burning

compost: to combine organic plant-based material that will decay into a mixture that can be used for fertilizing land

geothermal energy: energy that utilizes the heat of Earth's interior

hybrid-electric: a type of hybrid vehicle that combines a conventional internal combustion engine system with an electric propulsion system

fossil fuel: a fuel (such as coal, oil, or natural gas) formed in the earth from plant or animal remains

greenhouse gas: any of various gases (such as carbon dioxide or methane) that absorb infrared radiation, trap heat in the atmosphere, and contribute to the greenhouse effect

organic matter: material that has come from a recently living organism. It is capable of decay or is the product of decay.

maglev: short for magnetic levitation, a high-speed rail technology where the train is suspended on a magnetic cushion above a magnetized track and travels free of friction

mineralization: a process in which carbon dioxide is geologically stored by being converted to minerals via a series of chemical reactions

monocropping: the cultivation or growth of a single crop or organism, especially on agricultural or forested land

permaculture: an agricultural system or method that seeks to integrate human activity with natural surroundings to create highly efficient self-sustaining ecosystems

pesticides: an agent used to destroy pests, especially on crops

photosynthesis: the process by which plants and some bacteria use water and carbon dioxide to produce sugar for food

public transportation: a system of trains, buses, and other vehicles that is paid for or run by the government

partial zero emissions vehicle (PZEV): a more environmentally friendly, gas-powered vehicle that meets strict standards and produces no evaporative emissions

regenerative agriculture: a way of farming that focuses on soil health

renewable energy: energy that comes from unlimited, naturally replenished resources, such as the sun, tides, and wind

reservoir: a place for storing liquid, especially a natural or artificial lake providing water for a city or other area

Ring of Fire: a horseshoe-shaped region around the Pacific Ocean that's made up of many tectonic plates. More than 450 volcanoes (75 percent of the world's total) are found along the Ring of Fire.

sequestration: the process of capturing, securing, and storing something, such as carbon dioxide from the atmosphere

tectonic plate: one of the parts of Earth's surface that move in relation to each other

vegan: a person who consumes no food (such as meat, eggs, or dairy products) that comes from animals and does not use any animal products (such as leather)

vegetarian: a person who does not eat meat

SOURCE NOTES

20 "a house must . . . the same climate": Celeste Perron, "What Is a Passive House? The Next Big Thing in Eco-Friendly Building," Realtor.com, February 23, 2023, https://www.realtor.com/advice/buy/what-is-a-passive-house/.

26 "Public transit in . . . for a year.": Jen McGraw, "Public Transportation's Impacts on Greenhouse Gas Emissions," CNT, August 4, 2021, https://cnt.org/blog/public-transportations-impacts-on-greenhouse-gas-emissions.

28 "electric vehicles were . . . automobiles ever invented": Dave Roos, "Electric Vehicles Have Been Around Since the 19th Century: Timeline," History, April 15, 2024, https://www.history.com/news/electric-vehicles-automobiles-timeline.

51 "if food waste . . . US and China": Kelly Oakes, "How Cutting Your Food Waste Can Help the Climate," BBC, February 25, 2020, https://www.bbc.com/future/article/20200224-how-cutting-your-food-waste-can-help-the-climate.

SELECTED BIBLIOGRAPHY

Brady, Jeff. "Natural Gas Can Rival Coal's Climate-Warming Potential When Leaks are Counted." National Public Radio, July 14, 2023. https://www.npr.org/2023/07/14/1187648553/natural-gas-can-rival-coals-climate-warming-potential-when-leaks-are-counted.

Crownhart, Casey. "Yes, We Have Enough Materials to Power the World with Renewable Energy." *MIT Technology Review*, January 31, 2023. https://www.technologyreview.com/2023/01/31/1067444/we-have-enough-materials-to-power-world-with-renewables/.

Fisher, Adrian Ayres. "Native Shrubs and Why They're Essential for Carbon Sequestration." Resilience.org, January 2, 2019. https://www.resilience.org/stories/2019-01-02/native-shrubs-and-why-theyre-essential-for-carbon-sequestration/.

"Global Carbon Emissions from Fossil Fuels Reached Record High in 2023." *Stanford Doerr School of Sustainability*, December 5, 2023. https://sustainability.stanford.edu/news/global-carbon-emissions-fossil-fuels-reached-record-high-2023.

Henriques, Martha, and Zaria Gorvett. "The Climate Benefits of Veganism and Vegetarianism." BBC, May 1, 2022. https://www.bbc.com/future/article/20220429-the-climate-benefits-of-veganism-and-vegetarianism.

Lebling, Katie, and Eliza Northrop. "Leveraging the Ocean's Carbon Removal Potential." World Resources Institute, October 8, 2020. https://www.wri.org/insights/leveraging-oceans-carbon-removal-potential.

"New FAO Analysis Reveals Carbon Footprint of Agri-food Supply Chain." United Nations, November 8, 2021. https://news.un.org/en/story/2021/11/1105172.

Oakes, Kelly. "How Cutting Your Food Waste Can Help the Climate." BBC, February 25, 2020. https://www.bbc.com/future/article/20200224-how-cutting-your-food-waste-can-help-the-climate.

Robinson, Celeste, and Kate Huun. "The Impact of Recycling on Climate Change." University of Colorado Boulder Environmental Center, December 15, 2023. https://www.colorado.edu/ecenter/2023/12/15/impact-recycling-climate-change.

"Wind Farms Can Offset Their Emissions Within Two Years." *Science Daily*, May 16, 2024. https://www.sciencedaily.com/releases/2024/05/240516122608.htm.

FURTHER INFORMATION

BOOKS

Andra, Kayla. *Climate Change Modifications: How We Are Adapting*. Minneapolis: Twenty-First Century Books, 2026.
Learn what adaptation is, how scientists measure it, and the many ways groups, individuals, and the environment are already adapting in this thorough guide to climate change adaptation.

Davenport, Leslie. *All the Feelings Under the Sun: How to Deal with Climate Change*. Washington: Magination Press, 2021.
This book will help you deal with the emotions you might be feeling when learning about climate change. It will also introduce you to stories of young people who have helped to change the world, providing ideas and inspiration if you would like to do something about climate change.

Minoglio, Andrea. *Our World out of Balance: Understanding Climate Change and What We Can Do*. San Francisco: Blue Dot Kids, 2021.
Learn about air pollution, rising seas, plastic, waste, wildfires, and more. Then, explore more ways you can be a part of the solution to climate change.

Nardo, Don. *Climate Change Impact: Communities at Risk*. San Diego: ReferencePoint, 2025.
Dive into what climate change is and how it impacts the world in this guide. It covers extreme weather events, community displacement and adaptation, and more.

Schwartz, Heather E. *The Sunrise Movement: The Climate Revolution Generation*. Minneapolis: Lerner Publications, 2023.
This book spotlights the Sunrise Movement—a youth-led organization that is fighting the climate crisis worldwide. Learn the story of the young activists who created the movement and discover all the changes they have fought for and won.

WEBSITES

Climate Game

https://ig.ft.com/climate-game/

In this game developed by the *Financial Times*, your goal is to reach net zero carbon emissions by 2050. See if you can make the decisions necessary to combat climate change and explore solutions along the way.

Climate Kids

https://climatekids.nasa.gov/

From the National Aeronautics and Space Administration (NASA), Climate Kids has games, activities, and facts about climate change. Learn about weather and climate, the atmosphere, water, energy, plants, and animals. You can also investigate NASA missions that study these topics.

Kids Carbon Footprint Calculator: Learn to Live Eco-Friendly!

https://8billiontrees.com/carbon-offsets-credits/carbon-ecological-footprint-calculators/kids/

This interactive website allows you to calculate your own carbon footprint by considering transportation, food, energy, waste, and things in your home. Use this knowledge to figure out your impact on the environment.

A Student's Guide to Global Climate Change

https://archive.epa.gov/climatechange/kids/index.html

The EPA offers this guide, which allows you to investigate the aspects of climate change that interest you the most. It even allows you to take a virtual climate change expedition.

Sunrise Movement

https://www.sunrisemovement.org/

Delve into this youth-led organization and learn how you can participate in the fight against climate change.

INDEX

ABOUT THE AUTHOR

Rebecca Schroeder is a writer and science teacher living in the South Carolina low country. She studied Physics & Astronomy and Environmental Studies at the University of Pittsburgh, grounding her work in both scientific inquiry and environmental advocacy. A dual M.A. in International Affairs and Natural Resources & Sustainable Development from American University and the UN-Mandated University for Peace in Costa Rica brings a global perspective to Rebecca's writing. In her free time, she enjoys hiking, traveling, and stargazing.

PHOTO ACKNOWLEDGMENTS

WINDCOLORS/Shutterstock, cover; Arprince/Shutterstock, p.5; Edijs K/Shutterstock, p.7; Artur Nyk/Shutterstock, p.9; Tom Corcak/Shutterstock, p.11; Fahroni/Shutterstock, p.13; Andrew Will/Shutterstock, p.15; Ded Mityay/Shutterstock, p.17; Ermes Gunes/Shutterstock, p.19; Videoaniya/Shutterstock, p.21; HJUdall/Wikipedia Commons, p.23; IM Imagery/Shutterstock, p.25; Daan Verstraete/Shutterstock, p.27; Jackdude101/Wikimedia Commons, p.28; Christopher Moswitzer/Shutterstock, p.31; tororo reaction/Shutterstock, p.34; Wirestock Creators/Shutterstock, p.38; Jasmine Sahin/Shutterstock, p.39; Alchemist in India/Shutterstock, p.40; Pormezz/Shutterstock, p.42; 24K Production/Shutterstock, p.44; Fevziie/Shutterstock, p.45; AYO Production/Shutterstock, p.47; Jakub Rutkiewicz/Shutterstock, p.49; Ha-nu-man/Shutterstock, p.51; Aleksandar Malivuk/Shutterstock, p.52; DC Studio/Shutterstock, p.54.